CORNERSTONES
OF FREEDOM™

THE BOSTON TEA PARTY

BY KEVIN CUNNINGHAM

CHILDREN'S PRESS®

An Imprint of Scholastic Inc.

New York Toronto London Auckland Sydney

Mexico City New Delhi Hong Kong

Danbury, Connecticut

BRINGING HISTORY to LIFE

Content Consultant
James Marten, PhD
Professor and Chair, History Department
Marquette University
Milwaukee, Wisconsin

Library of Congress Cataloging-in-Publication Data

Cunningham, Kevin, 1966–
  The Boston Tea Party/by Kevin Cunningham.
       pages cm.—(Cornerstones of freedom)
  Includes bibliographical references and index.
  ISBN-13: 978-0-531-23051-0 (lib. bdg.)
  ISBN-13: 978-0-531-28151-2 (pbk.)
  1. Boston Tea Party, 1773—Juvenile literature. I. Title.
  E215.7.C86 2012
  973.3'115—dc23   2012000495

  2 3 4 5 6 7 8 9 10 R 22 21 20 19 18 17 16 15 14 13

Photographs © 2013: Alamy Images: 35 (2d Alan King), 27 (Ivy Close
Images); AP Images/North Wind Picture Archives: 28 (Alonso Chappel),
5 top, 7, 12, 22, 23, 42, 45, 46, 47, 57 top; Bridgeman Art Library: 49 (Clyde
Osmer Deland/© Philadelphia History Museum at the Atwater Kent/
Courtesy of Historical Society of Pennsylvania Collection), 30 (John
Singleton Copley/Private Collection/Peter Newark American Pictures),
cover, 39 (Private Collection/Peter Newark American Pictures), 10 (Richard
Houston/Leeds Museums and Galleries U.K.), 18 (Robert Salmon/U.S. Naval
Academy, Annapolis, Maryland); Getty Images: 20, 56 (Stock Montage),
4 top, 37, 41 (The Bridgeman Art Library), 50, 59 (Time & Life Pictures);
Superstock, Inc.: 55 (Eugene Hess), 4 bottom, 16 (Fine Art Images), 40;
Courtesy of The Bostonian Society/The Old State House Museum: 38, 51;
The Granger Collection: 24 (Charles Willson Peale), 25, 57 bottom (John
Singleton Copley), back cover, 2, 3, 5 bottom, 6, 13, 14, 15, 17, 21, 26, 32, 33,
38, 58; The Image Works/The British Library: 8.

Maps by XNR Productions, Inc.

Did you know that studying history can be fun?

BRING HISTORY TO LIFE by becoming a history investigator. Examine the evidence (primary and secondary source materials); cross-examine the people and witnesses. Take a look at what was happening at the time—but be careful! What happened years ago might suddenly become incredibly interesting and change the way you think!

Contents

4

Paying for Victory

Great Britain won the French and Indian War, but the cost of victory was high, both in terms of money spent and loss of life.

In 1754, Great Britain, its American colonies, and their Native American allies went to war with France and its Native American allies. The French and Indian War raged until 1763. That year, France turned ownership of its colony in Canada over to Great Britain.

THE FRENCH AND INDIAN WAR WAS

The war gave Great Britain control of eastern North America. But victory was expensive. The British government had borrowed money to pay for soldiers and supplies. The country began to have trouble paying its bills. Meanwhile, rivals surrounded the American colonies. French settlers remained in Canada. Unfriendly Native American peoples lived to the west. Spain held land in the far western part of the continent.

Great Britain left 10,000 soldiers in America after the war to protect the colonies from attacks. But the soldiers and their forts cost yet more money. Britain's government needed to somehow find a source of **revenue** to help pay for them. Their decisions would lead to an event known more than 200 years later as the Boston Tea Party.

French settlements remained in Canada even after the French and Indian War.

CHAPTER 1

A PROBLEM with TAXES

Enslaved Africans provided most of the labor on Caribbean sugar plantations.

ONE PRODUCT THAT PLAYED a major role in colonial trade was **molasses**. Sugar growers on Caribbean islands sold it to rum makers in the colonies. Once the molasses was turned into rum, the drink was shipped to Africa. Traders in Africa swapped the rum and other products for enslaved people. Ships then carried the African slaves to European colonies in the Caribbean and North America. British law stated that American colonists could only buy molasses from British sugar growers. But colonists had long dodged the law by **smuggling** cheap molasses into North America. In 1764, British prime minister George Grenville hoped to address the smuggling problem by introducing a new law.

British prime minister
Grenville considered
smuggling a major
problem in the colonies.

Unhappy Colonists

Parliament passed a new law called the Sugar Act. It cut
the old molasses tax in half and placed taxes on coffee
and other products. It also stated that the colonists
could sell lumber and iron only to Great Britain. Cutting
the old tax in half might have pleased the colonists.
But Grenville also ordered Britain's navy to stop the
smuggling. Colonial rum makers soon began to go out
of business. The lumber and farm goods that had been
traded for molasses no longer had buyers. Farmers,

lumbermen, and the merchants whose ships carried their products struggled.

This loss of business came at a bad time. The colonial economy was in a slump. Many people had trouble paying bills and finding work. Colonists blamed the Sugar Act for the bad economy, though this was not the actual cause. They also became more suspicious of the British soldiers stationed in North America. They believed that Parliament might use the soldiers to force them to pay the new taxes.

A VIEW FROM ABROAD

Members of Parliament believed that the colonists should pay taxes to cover some of the cost of the soldiers protecting them. British subjects living in Great Britain paid heavy taxes, and British officials believed that colonists should do the same. No one considered it a way to solve Britain's money problems. Prime Minister George Grenville realized that the money raised by the Sugar Act wouldn't even cover the cost of the troops.

The tax itself was not the only issue. Smuggling cost the British government money. Even worse, much of the smuggled molasses came from France, Great Britain's long-time rival.

Officials in several colonies complained to members of Parliament. They suggested that the Sugar Act was illegal. They believed that colonists should only pay taxes passed by their elected government representatives. Because colonists had no representatives in Parliament, they believed that Parliament could not legally tax the colonies. The colonists called this "taxation without representation." The members of Parliament disagreed. They considered themselves representatives of all British subjects, including colonists.

Stamps and Taxes

Parliament passed a new tax called the Stamp Act on March 22, 1765. The Stamp Act forced colonists to buy stamps for printed papers such as newspapers, legal documents, and playing cards. Not all members of Parliament agreed with this new tax. But Grenville

The Stamp Act required colonists to purchase stamps for almost all printed documents.

News of the Stamp Act angered many colonists.

and his allies outvoted them. Word soon reached the colonies that the Stamp Act would go into effect on November 1.

Virginia's **legislature**, the House of Burgesses, acted first. Patrick Henry led a vote on May 30 approving four statements called the Virginia Resolves. The resolves

A FIRSTHAND LOOK AT
THE VIRGINIA RESOLVES

The Virginia Resolves was one of the earliest official statements against taxation without representation. See page 60 for a link to view the original document online.

Patrick Henry was one of the first colonial leaders to speak out against the Stamp Act.

argued that Virginians should be taxed only by their own representatives in the House of Burgesses. Virginia's governor was an official appointed by Great Britain. He refused to approve the resolves. But Henry's words stirred up anger.

Throughout the colonies, crowds marched against the Stamp Act. There were threats and even attacks on British officials and supporters of the act. The New York stamp agent resigned after a mob destroyed his house. New Hampshire's stamp agent hid on a ship. New Jersey stamp agent William Coxe gave up the job even before he received threats. In seaside towns, ships carrying stamps weren't allowed to dock.

Protesters organized into groups to better fight the Stamp Act. Patriot groups using the name the Sons of Liberty appeared in many places. Some colonists began a **boycott** of British products. In October 1765, representatives from nine colonies held a Stamp Act

Stamp Act protests quickly became common throughout the colonies.

STAMP ACT

THE FOLLY OF ENGLAND
THE RUIN OF AMERICA

The representatives of the Stamp Act Congress presented arguments to persuade King George III (above) that the Stamp Act was unfair.

Congress in New York City. They drew up a document listing their complaints and sent it to Parliament and King George III.

The Right Kind of Taxes

Colonists accepted that they had to pay taxes passed by their legislatures. The problem was taxation without representation. The colonists believed that if Parliament got away with the Stamp Act, more taxes would follow.

The violent protests against the act angered many members of Parliament. Some wanted to keep the tax to show power over the colonies. Others took the colonists' side.

A loss of business in Great Britain solved the argument in Parliament. The American boycott left British merchants unable to sell products in the colonies. Merchants put pressure on members of Parliament as they lost money. Parliament **repealed** the Stamp Act in March 1766. Ships brought the news to the colonies in May. Celebrations broke out everywhere. But the struggle over taxation without representation was far from over.

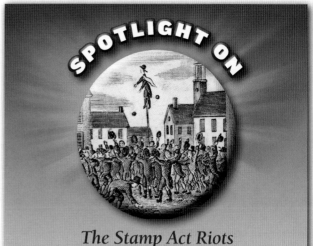

SPOTLIGHT ON

The Stamp Act Riots

Much of the Stamp Act violence took place in Boston, Massachusetts. A group of workers and shop owners called the Loyal Nine organized a gang that harassed Andrew Oliver, the Massachusetts stamp agent. On August 14, 1765, the Loyal Nine hung a dummy of Oliver from an elm they called the Liberty Tree.

Thomas Hutchinson, the lieutenant governor and head of the courts for Massachusetts, told a sheriff to cut down the dummy. But a crowd refused to let the sheriff pass. Over the course of the next day, the mob burned the dummy, destroyed an office building Oliver owned, and wrecked the inside of Oliver's house. Oliver agreed to resign. Another mob attacked Hutchinson's house at the end of August. People stole what they could carry. The rest of the property was damaged or destroyed.

CHAPTER 2

CRADLE of LIBERTY

Boston was one of the busiest ports in the colonies.

BOSTON RELIED HEAVILY ON

shipping. Dozens of **wharves** jutted out from its shoreline. Products such as lumber and food were shipped to Great Britain from Boston's ports. British products such as glass and paint were returned on the ships and unloaded by Boston workers. Boston merchants owned the ships and took a share of the money going both ways. They had good business reasons for opposing taxes. The merchants and many others in the city were hit hard by the new taxes. From the beginning, Boston was a center of antitax protest.

Samuel Adams became an important leader in the struggle against unfair taxation.

Samuel Adams

One of Boston's loudest voices against British taxes belonged to Samuel Adams. Adams had once worked as a tax collector. He became popular for not collecting money.

During the Stamp Act protests, Adams wrote and spoke about resisting British taxes. He stood against violent protests, though he may have been friends with some of those people involved in such protests. He believed that violent acts gave Parliament an excuse not to listen. He wanted to show Great Britain that colonists had a legal right to fight unfair taxes even if it meant **rebellion**.

Boston voters elected Adams to the Massachusetts House of Representatives in 1765. This position gave his words new power. He wrote a list of resolves declaring Massachusetts's rights. He also became an ally of James Otis Jr., a House leader and a member of the Sons of Liberty.

Boston merchant John Hancock joined Adams and Otis in the Boston Assembly the following spring. He soon jumped into a leadership position among those opposed to British taxes. These people became known as Patriots. They believed that the colonies deserved more rights to govern themselves.

TODAY'S PERSPECTIVE

Historians once believed that Samuel Adams encouraged violence such as the Stamp Act riots. They thought that he controlled the mobs in Boston and used them to get his way. But many of today's historians disagree. They think that the mobs worked against Adams's wishes. Some historians believe Adams's goal was to convince the British that the colonists had rights that Parliament should recognize. Violence only encouraged Parliament to punish the colonists instead of listening to them.

The Townshend Acts

The Patriot movement faced a new challenge in 1767. Parliament passed a new series of laws that colonists referred to as the Townshend Acts. These unpopular laws included taxes suggested by a British official named Charles Townshend.

The Revenue Act was the first of the Townshend Acts. It taxed glass, paint, tea, and other important products the colonists had to **import** from Britain. It also gave the authorities the right to search for smuggled goods on colonists' property. Townshend's goal for the Revenue Act was not to make money. His point was to show the colonies that Parliament could tax them.

Charles Townshend hoped that by imposing new taxes he would prove once and for all that the colonies were under control of the British Parliament.

The Townshend Acts gave British soldiers the power to invade colonists' homes and businesses to search for smuggled goods.

Pennsylvania lawyer John Dickinson wrote essays against the Revenue Act. He argued thoughtfully against taxation without representation. His calm words were a contrast to the violence that followed the Stamp Act. Dickinson believed that it was better to use words than violence to convince Parliament to end taxation.

The Soldiers Arrive

Great Britain assigned inspectors to collect the new taxes. But Boston merchants refused to let the inspectors board their ships. An attempt to secretly search one of Hancock's ships ended with Hancock and some of his employees carrying the inspector off the boat. Inspectors later struck back by taking one of Hancock's ships. A mob pelted the British troops with stones as the British

John Dickinson attempted to convince the colonists that violence would not help them resolve their problems.

pulled the ship away. Then the crowd turned on the inspectors. One was beaten. Others had their homes attacked.

To prevent these sorts of attacks from happening again, the British government sent 1,000 soldiers into Boston on October 2, 1768. Angry Bostonians watched as the troops set up their camps. Meanwhile, British warships stood in a line with their guns pointed at the city. The customs inspectors, now with armed soldiers behind them, began to check every ship going in or out of the city's ports.

The British army in Boston soon grew to about 4,000 men. The sound of drums and marching troops announced

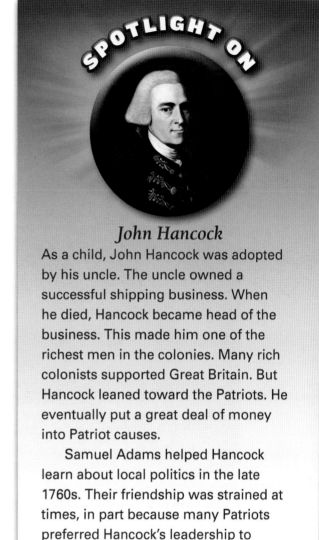

SPOTLIGHT ON

John Hancock

As a child, John Hancock was adopted by his uncle. The uncle owned a successful shipping business. When he died, Hancock became head of the business. This made him one of the richest men in the colonies. Many rich colonists supported Great Britain. But Hancock leaned toward the Patriots. He eventually put a great deal of money into Patriot causes.

Samuel Adams helped Hancock learn about local politics in the late 1760s. Their friendship was strained at times, in part because many Patriots preferred Hancock's leadership to Adams's. But the two brought their followers together during major clashes with Great Britain. Hancock later served as governor of Massachusetts from 1780 to 1785 and from 1787 to 1793.

Large numbers of British soldiers began flooding into Boston in 1768.

the soldiers' presence. The people of Boston were not welcoming to their new neighbors. Patriots refused to hire off-duty soldiers for part-time jobs. Merchants organized another boycott of British goods.

Fights between Patriots and pro-British Tories became common. A Patriot gang dressed as Mohawk

Indians made trouble in taverns. Others beat soldiers caught alone on the street. One fight left James Otis with permanent injuries.

The bad feelings turned worse when a merchant loyal to the Tories shot and killed an 11-year-old boy. Around 5,000 Bostonians followed behind the boy's coffin as it was taken to the cemetery.

The Tories were made fun of by many colonists.

Tensions between colonists and British soldiers erupted in the Boston Massacre.

The Boston Massacre

On March 5, 1770, a crowd of workers and young boys faced off against eight British soldiers on Boston's King

Street. The Bostonians threw ice balls, oyster shells, and garbage at the soldiers. Then someone threw a club, which knocked one of the soldiers off balance. Shots rang out. Five men died of gunshot wounds during the fight. Six more people were injured. The incident became known as the Boston **Massacre**.

Governor Thomas Hutchinson told Bostonians, "The law shall have its course." He promised to try the King Street soldiers for murder. Hancock, Hutchinson, and other leaders met to find a solution to the violence. The British agreed to pull the troops out of Boston. Troublemakers continued to try to gather mobs. But a group of citizens volunteered to patrol the streets and prevent trouble. One was lawyer and future U.S. president John Adams.

On the same day as the Boston Massacre, Parliament canceled the Townshend Acts. Great Britain would no longer collect taxes on any of the goods named in the Revenue Act, except for one. It had refused to lift the tax on tea.

CHAPTER 3

A MAGNIFICENT MOVEMENT

British officials temporarily drew John Hancock away from Patriot activities by placing him in charge of other important projects.

TROUBLE IN THE COLONIES

eased for a few years after the Townshend Acts were lifted. American merchants soon imported British goods again. British officials tried to tempt John Hancock and other rich merchants away from the Patriots. Governor Thomas Hutchinson even made Hancock leader of the city's **militia**, the Corps of Cadets. For a time, Hancock put his energy toward the corps and other projects. He bought a fire engine for Boston and organized the purchase of new street lamps that burned whale oil. But a new tax would soon draw him back to the Patriot cause.

The Tea Act gave the British East India Company the exclusive right to trade tea to the colonies.

The Tea Act

Parliament passed the Tea Act in May 1773. It stated that only the British East India Company could trade tea to the American colonies. In addition, the company did not have to pay the tea tax. That allowed it to sell tea cheaper than colonial merchants could.

The Sons of Liberty took to the newspapers to argue against the Tea Act. By fall, more colonists had begun to protest the act. Merchants in Philadelphia, Pennsylvania, and New York City gave in to threats from protesters and stopped trading with the East India Company. River pilots were told not to bring tea ships into Philadelphia—or else.

In October, Samuel Adams and others launched newspaper attacks on merchants selling the East India Company's tea. The merchants struck back in another paper. Adams called a town meeting at the Liberty Tree to demand that the merchants resign. When they refused, the Sons of Liberty attacked a warehouse belonging to merchant Richard Clarke. A second meeting failed to convince the merchants. So did damaging Clarke's house.

The *Dartmouth*

The *Dartmouth* was a 79-foot-long (24-meter-long) American ship owned by the Rotch family of Massachusetts. On November 28, it arrived in Boston

The Liberty Tree was a popular meeting place for Patriots in the years leading up to the American Revolution.

Harbor carrying 114 chests of tea belonging to the East India Company. Church bells all over Boston began to ring the next morning to signal an emergency. Not everyone who joined the crowds streaming down the streets knew what was going on.

Five thousand people met in the Old South Meeting House. The two-day meeting ended with demands that the tea stay on the *Dartmouth* and that all tea ships return to Britain.

The *Dartmouth* docked at Griffin's Wharf in early December. Bostonians stood guard to make sure that no one unloaded the tea from the *Dartmouth* or the two other tea ships that were waiting in the port.

Francis Rotch, part owner of the *Dartmouth*, wanted the tea off his ship. The law said that he had 20 days to unload

Despite the colonists' protests, the *Dartmouth* carried East India Company tea into Boston Harbor.

and pay a **duty** on the cargo. If he failed, the authorities could take his goods and his ship. Rotch also needed to clear the cargo out of the *Dartmouth* so that he could use the ship to take whale oil to Great Britain for sale.

Other people had their own reasons for wanting the tea off the ship. The tea merchants would have to pay for the tea if it failed to be unloaded.

Taking Sides

December 16 was the deadline to pay the duty on the tea. That day, Rotch asked for permission to take the tea back to Great Britain. British officials refused. The same day, 5,000 protesters again filled the Old South Meeting

House. The leaders of the meeting told Rotch to demand a special pass to leave the harbor.

Rotch was gone all afternoon. The restless crowd listened to speeches to pass the time. Rotch finally returned at 5:45 p.m. He announced that Governor Hutchinson would not give him the special pass. The tired crowd surged to life. "This meeting can do nothing more to save the country," Samuel Adams cried.

Fifteen or 20 minutes later, a small group of men disguised as Mohawk Indians led the way to Griffin's Wharf. A quiet crowd followed some distance behind them. Other "Mohawks" joined the group as it marched through the streets. The Boston Tea Party had begun.

The Mysterious "Mohawks"

Patriot leaders had planned ahead of time. The 20 or so "Mohawks" had even prepared their disguises. Many of these men, such as George Hewes, were trusted veterans of past protests. They wrapped themselves in blankets and smeared soot on their faces.

A FIRSTHAND LOOK AT
JOHN ADAMS'S LETTER

Many colonists were certain that the tea would successfully be sent back to Great Britain. Among them was John Adams. Just five days before the Boston Tea Party, Adams drafted a letter to government officials, writing that "The Tea Ships are all to return, whatever may be the Consequence." See page 60 for a link to read the entire letter online.

The Patriots dressed as Mohawk Indians so that British officials would not recognize them.

The disguises had nothing to do with tricking the British. No Mohawk Indians lived anywhere near Boston. Instead, the men feared being identified. What they intended to do aboard the ships was illegal. If caught, the men could land in jail or be sent overseas for hard labor. The British could even charge them with **treason**. The penalty for treason was death.

Historians today are unsure just who was at the Boston Tea Party. But we know Patriot leaders warned Samuel Adams that the Mohawks should not get out of control. The theft and destruction seen in past protests were forbidden. Adams listened. He knew that

Thomas Melvill is one of the few men later identified as having participated in the Boston Tea Party.

the Patriots needed some of Boston's wealthy merchants on their side. Only responsible, trustworthy Patriots boarded the tea ships. Others who joined the Mohawks on the way to the wharf followed their lead. Evidence suggests that a few educated professionals such as doctors and merchants took part in the Boston Tea Party. One participant, Thomas Melvill, was a businessman with two college degrees. Several more seem to have had careers as skilled workers. Hewes was a shoemaker. Thomas Crafts worked as a painter. Farmers from towns near Boston also may have played a role.

Choosing men who were less well known made it easier for them to keep their identities secret. Some participants may even have been teenagers.

All Aboard

The Corps of Cadets guarded the tea ships. They expected the Mohawks and let them pass. Patriot leaders quickly divided the 200 or so men present into three groups. At around 7 p.m., each group boarded a tea ship. The leader of Hewes's group told him to ask the ship's captain for the keys to the storage areas and for candles. The captain handed over both. He also asked Hewes to make sure the men did not damage his ship. Then the Patriots went to work. Hewes remembered, "We then were ordered by our commander to open the hatches, and take out all the chests of tea and throw them overboard, and we immediately proceeded to execute his orders; first cutting and splitting the chests with our tomahawks, so as thoroughly to expose them to the effects of the water."

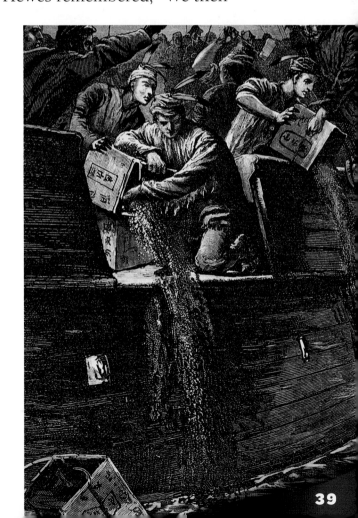

The Patriots dumped more than 300 crates of tea into the waters of Boston Harbor.

People on the dock watched as the Patriots threw tea from the ship.

Joshua Wyeth, a 16-year-old blacksmith, said, "We were merry . . . at the idea of making so large a cup of tea for the fishes."

The men on the ships remained as quiet as possible. So did the thousand or so people watching from shore. Armed British ships sat nearby. Redcoats patrolled the streets. No one wanted a fight. Tea chests were cracked open with axes and splashed into the harbor for the next two or three hours.

The volunteers touched nothing other than tea and hurt no one. One of the ship's crew may have even received a lock to replace one that was broken by accident. The Patriots destroyed 342 tea chests in all. That came to about 90,000 pounds (40,823 kg) of tea worth around one million of today's dollars.

The Morning After

Samuel Adams and Boston's other Patriot leaders hoped the tea protest would bring the colonies together against Britain. Patriot Paul Revere rode to Philadelphia on December 17 to spread word of the Boston Tea Party.

Tea agents resigned from the East India Company in Philadelphia; New York City; and Charleston, South Carolina. On Christmas Day, 8,000 people near Philadelphia forced a tea ship to turn around. The Sons of Liberty in New York City vowed to do the same.

"This is the most magnificent movement of all," John Adams wrote in his diary. He predicted the destruction of the tea would one day be seen as a major event in history.

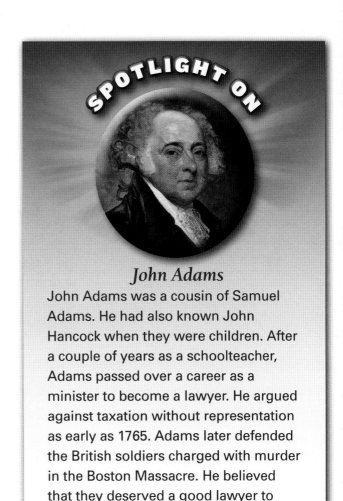

SPOTLIGHT ON

John Adams

John Adams was a cousin of Samuel Adams. He had also known John Hancock when they were children. After a couple of years as a schoolteacher, Adams passed over a career as a minister to become a lawyer. He argued against taxation without representation as early as 1765. Adams later defended the British soldiers charged with murder in the Boston Massacre. He believed that they deserved a good lawyer to prove the colonies could hold a fair trial. During the trial, he made his famous statement, "Facts are stubborn things."

CHAPTER 4

AFTER THE TEA PARTY

Prime Minister Frederick North reacted to the Boston Tea Party by strengthening efforts to prove British authority over the colonies.

NEWS OF THE TEA PARTY

reached Great Britain in January. The news shocked and angered the king, members of Parliament, and London's citizens. The British saw the colonists as misbehaving children. Officials declared that they needed to be punished. Parliament was determined to bring the colonists in line once and for all. "We are now to dispute the question whether we have, or have not any authority in that country," said Prime Minister Frederick North. Great Britain meant to prove that it did indeed have authority over the colonists.

A VIEW FROM ABROAD

The Boston Tea Party turned Great Britain against the Patriots. Even people once in favor of the colonies' rights considered the tea party to be destruction of property. Some even believed that dumping the tea was an act of rebellion against the king. The government soon charged John Hancock and Samuel Adams with treason. But British officials had no proof that they were involved. The charges were ignored until April 19, 1775, when British forces attempted to arrest the two men. Colonial forces prevented the arrest, leading to the first battle of the Revolutionary War.

Hancock's Speech

Protests continued through winter and spring. In March 1774, "Mohawks" dumped tea that had been hidden in a shop. New York's Sons of Liberty held their own tea party the next month.

Bostonians observed the anniversary of the Boston Massacre on March 5. A larger-than-usual crowd filled the Old South Meeting House to hear John Hancock speak.

Hancock started out quietly. Then his voice became stronger as he called the British "bloody butchers" and "murderers." Hancock made two important suggestions in his speech. He said that towns in Massachusetts should organize armed militias ready to act when danger calls. He also stated that the colonies needed to unite.

A FIRSTHAND LOOK AT
JOHN HANCOCK'S SPEECH

A huge crowd gathered at the Old South Meeting House on March 5, 1774. Most people were not there to remember the Boston Massacre, but to hear what John Hancock had to say about the Boston Tea Party. See page 60 for a link to read the text of Hancock's speech online.

No other American leader had ever made such a statement in public. The rich merchant with so much to lose had said that he stood with the Patriots, no matter what happened.

After the Boston Tea Party, John Hancock's criticism of the British government grew even stronger.

The Intolerable Acts

Parliament passed laws in the spring of 1774 to punish Boston for the tea party. Patriots referred to the laws as the **Intolerable** Acts.

The Boston Port Act halted all trade in Boston Harbor. The law had a severe effect. Boston's economy depended on shipping. Bostonians lost their jobs. Food and other important goods became scarce and expensive. Under the Boston Port Act, the harbor could only reopen if Massachusetts repaid the East India Company for the lost tea.

A second act took away the right of Massachusetts to select many of its own government officials. It also restricted Bostonians to only one town meeting per year. Another act

A LIST of the Names of those who AUDACIOUSLY continue to counteract the UNITED SENTIMENTS of the BODY of Merchants thro'out NORTH-AMERICA; by importing British Goods contrary to the Agreement.

John Bernard,
(In King-Street, almost opposite Vernon's Head.

James McMasters,
(On Treat's Wharf.

Patrick McMasters,
(Opposite the Sign of the Lamb.

John Mein,
(Opposite the White-Horse, and in King-Street.

Nathaniel Rogers,
(Opposite Mr. Henderson Inches Store lower End King-Street.

William Jackson,
At the Brazen Head, Cornhill, near the Town-House.

Theophilus Lillie,
(Near Mr. Pemberton's Meeting-House, North-End.

John Taylor,
(Nearly opposite the Heart and Crown in Cornhill.

Ame & Elizabeth Cummings,
(Opposite the Old Brick Meeting-House, all of Boston.

Israel Williams, Esq; & Son,
(Traders in the Town of Hatfield.

And, Henry Barnes,
(Trader in the Town of M toro'.

Patriots published the names of merchants who cooperated with the British so colonists would boycott those businesses.

The Intolerable Acts forced Boston's citizens to make space for British soldiers to live in their homes.

stated that any British official accused of serious crimes would be moved out of Massachusetts for a trial. Yet another forced colonial authorities to provide quarters for British soldiers, even if it meant putting them in private homes.

General Thomas Gage replaced Thomas Hutchinson as governor. He brought in extra troops to keep order. The British soon began to behave as if Boston were a conquered enemy city.

Coming Together

Throughout the summer patriots in other colonies gathered to take action. Secret meetings outside of British

YESTERDAY'S HEADLINES

Not all colonists supported the Boston Tea Party. Some criticized it, including colonists who disliked the British taxes. Even George Washington (above) disagreed strongly with the Bostonians' actions. In Massachusetts, farmers outside Boston blamed city troublemakers for angering the British. The farmers depended on British customers. Leaders in the South also disapproved of the destruction of other people's property. The southern colonies had ceased anti-British actions after Britain canceled the Townshend Acts.

control took the place of the legislatures. Such groups soon began organizing colonists into militias, as Hancock had suggested. His call for a congress also found listeners. All of the colonies except Georgia agreed to send representatives to a Continental Congress in September 1774.

Sympathy for Boston grew. Patriots in Windham, Connecticut, sent 258 sheep to feed hungry Bostonians. Towns from all over the colonies gave gifts of meat, grain, and other supplies. Bostonians glared angrily at the British Redcoats around them. The soldiers on patrol made sure to stay in groups. Lone soldiers were at risk of being attacked by the colonists.

In September, Massachusetts sent its four representatives to Philadelphia for the Continental

Congress. Samuel Adams, John Adams, Thomas Cushing, and Robert Treat Paine left for Philadelphia under the watch of British troops. Hancock stayed behind to lead the Patriots.

The Continental Congress met on September 5. Never before had the colonies come together in such a way. The representatives discussed many issues. By the end of the meeting in October, the 12 colonies attending had agreed to boycott British goods. They also planned to meet again the following May.

Leaders from across the colonies traveled to Philadelphia for the First Continental Congress.

Old Memories

For a long time, most people did not consider the Boston Tea Party an important event. It did not even have a name. The term "Boston Tea Party" probably wasn't used in print until the 1830s.

Participants were careful not to talk about the tea party too much. British officials could still have charged them with crimes such as destruction of property. Those who discussed the events in Boston Harbor often told their stories only to children, grandchildren, and trusted friends.

The threat eased as time passed. The surviving tea party participants began to tell their stories. Americans became interested in details about the revolution during the 1820s. Writers, journalists, and historians set out to find people who had taken part in these past events.

Hewes Returns

Two authors tracked down and interviewed George Hewes during the 1830s. Hewes was in his 90s by then. Each of the authors later wrote a book about Hewes's life.

Decades after the American Revolution, when people studied the war, they also took a closer look at the events of the Boston Tea Party.

George Hewes's firsthand account of the Boston Tea Party helped spread awareness of the event.

James Hawkes published his book about Hewes in 1834. Hewes and his youngest son took a trip to Boston the next year. On the way, Hewes was interviewed by a Rhode Island newspaper. His story also made the papers in Boston. A local artist painted his portrait. On the Fourth of July, he rode in the parade and sat at a dinner in his honor. Benjamin Thatcher released the second book about Hewes at the end of the year.

The story of the Boston Tea Party soon took on a new importance to many Americans. Today, we see the destruction of the tea as a major event in American history, just as John Adams predicted.

What Happened Where?

...hn Hancock's House
...e wealthy merchant and Patriot John
...ncock lived in one of Boston's finest
...ses. The building was destroyed in 1863.
...t of the Massachusetts State House now
...on the site.

...South Meeting House
...e Old South Meeting House hosted the
...or meetings that took place before the
...party. Built in 1729, it remains one of
...ton's most famous buildings.

...e of the Boston Liberty Tree
...ing the Stamp Act protests, Boston
...riots selected a large elm as the Liberty
...e. The Liberty Tree was an important
...eting place during the late 1760s and
...0s. The elm is gone now. A plaque
...wing its former location is on a building
...30 Washington Street.

Liberty
■ Tree

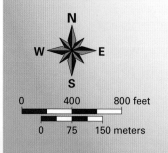

N
W · E
S

```
0        400        800 feet
```
```
0      75      150 meters
```

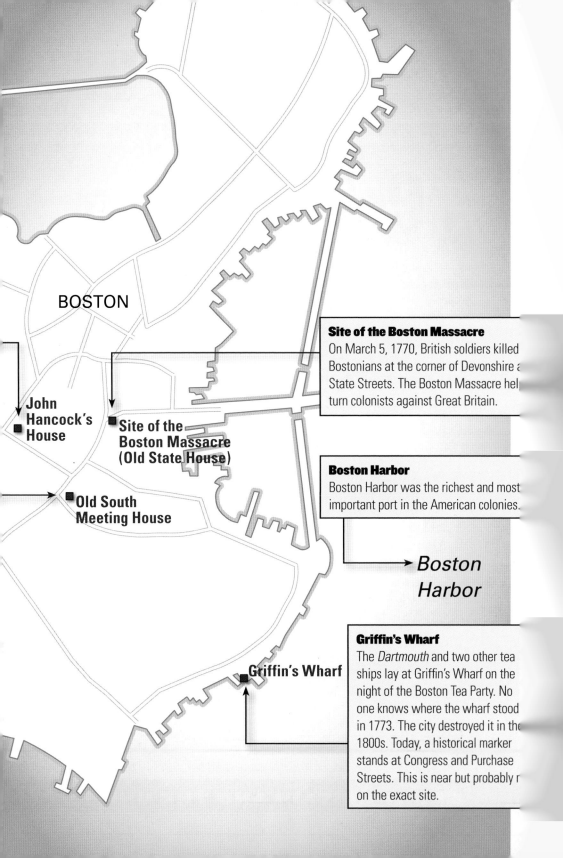

BOSTON

Site of the Boston Massacre
On March 5, 1770, British soldiers killed
Bostonians at the corner of Devonshire a
State Streets. The Boston Massacre hel
turn colonists against Great Britain.

John
Hancock's
House

Site of the
Boston Massacre
(Old State House)

Boston Harbor
Boston Harbor was the richest and most
important port in the American colonies.

Old South
Meeting House

→ *Boston
Harbor*

Griffin's Wharf
The *Dartmouth* and two other tea
ships lay at Griffin's Wharf on the
night of the Boston Tea Party. No
one knows where the wharf stood
in 1773. The city destroyed it in the
1800s. Today, a historical marker
stands at Congress and Purchase
Streets. This is near but probably n
on the exact site.

Griffin's Wharf

Thirteen Colonies, One Nation

In October 1774, the Continental Congress met to form the first American government totally free of British control. Hancock was elected president of the Congress. The Congress began to buy supplies for a new Continental army. It also created the minutemen, soldiers ready for action "at a minute's warning."

On April 19, 1775, the Massachusetts militia battled British troops at Lexington and Concord outside Boston. The fighting marked the start of the Revolutionary War. The Second Continental Congress began to discuss independence from Britain in spring 1776. The representatives voted in favor of it on July 2. The Congress approved the Declaration of Independence two days later. Hancock signed his name in large letters. Samuel Adams, John Adams, and other colonial leaders added their signatures.

The war raged until 1781. That October, George Washington's Continental army and its French allies trapped a British army at Yorktown, Virginia. Parliament decided to end the fighting. The last British troops left two years later. After a long, tumultuous period, the 13 colonies became the United States of America.

The British surrender at Yorktown effectively ended the Revolutionary War.

STATES SIGNED A PEACE TREATY IN 1783.

INFLUENTIAL INDIVIDUALS

Samuel Adams

Thomas Hutchinson (1711–1780) was the governor of Massachusetts and an opponent of the Patriot movement.

George Grenville (1712–1770) was the leader of Britain's government during passage of the Sugar Act and Stamp Act.

Thomas Gage (1721–1787) was a British general in charge of keeping peace in Boston in the early 1770s.

Samuel Adams (1722–1803) was a Boston politician and Patriot leader.

Charles Townshend (1725–1767) was a British politician who led the effort to pass the Townshend Acts.

James Otis Jr. (1725–1783) was a Boston lawyer and Patriot leader.

Frederick North (1732–1792) was prime minister of Great Britain at the time of the Boston Tea Party.

John Adams (1735–1826) was a Boston lawyer and Patriot.

Patrick Henry (1736–1799) was a Virginia Patriot and author of the Virginia Resolves.

John Hancock (1737–1793) was a Boston merchant and Patriot leader who served as president of the Second Continental Congress.

George Hewes (1742–1840) was a Boston shoemaker who took part in the Boston Tea Party. His account of the tea party later helped establish the event as an important part of history.

Frederick North

John Hancock

TIMELINE

1763

The French and Indian War ends.

1764

Parliament passes the Sugar Act.

1770

March 5
The Boston Massacre takes place.

1773

May
Parliament passes the Tea Act.

November 28
The *Dartmouth*, a tea ship, arrives in Boston.

December 16
The Boston Tea Party takes place.

1765

March 22
Parliament passes the Stamp Act.

May 30
Virginia's House of Burgesses passes the Virginia Resolves opposing the Stamp Act.

1767

Parliament passes the first of the Townshend Acts.

1774

The first of the Intolerable Acts becomes law.

1775

April 19
The Revolutionary War begins with the Battles of Lexington and Concord.

LIVING HISTORY

Primary sources provide firsthand evidence about a topic. Witnesses to a historical event create primary sources. They include autobiographies, newspaper reports of the time, oral histories, photographs, and memoirs. A secondary source analyzes primary sources, and is one step or more removed from the event. Secondary sources include textbooks, encyclopedias, and commentaries.

To view the following primary and secondary sources, go to www.factsfornow.scholastic.com. Enter the keywords **Boston Tea Party** and look for the Living History logo ⅀ᵢ.

⅀ᵢ **The Boston Massacre Trial** More than 40 witnesses wrote accounts of the Boston Massacre to be read in court.

⅀ᵢ **John Adams's Letter** John Adams's December 11, 1773, letter shows that he believed the tea ships in Boston would soon return to England.

⅀ᵢ **John Hancock's Speech** On the first anniversary of the Boston Massacre, John Hancock gave a speech in which he defended the Boston Tea Party and made it clear he stood with the Patriots against Great Britain.

⅀ᵢ **The Virginia Resolves** Patrick Henry wrote several versions of the Virginia Resolves.

RESOURCES

Books

Fradin, Dennis. *The Boston Tea Party*. New York: Marshall Cavendish Benchmark, 2008.

Gibson, Karen Bush. *The Life and Times of Samuel Adams*. Hockessin, DE: Mitchell Lane, 2007.

Gondosch, Linda. *How Did Tea and Taxes Spark a Revolution? And Other Questions About the Boston Tea Party*. Minneapolis: Lerner, 2011.

Visit this Scholastic Web site for more information on the Boston Tea Party: www.factsfornow.scholastic.com Enter the keywords Boston Tea Party

GLOSSARY

boycott (BOI-kaht) a refusal to buy goods from a person, group, or country

duty (DOO-tee) a tax on imported goods

import (im-PORT) to bring in from a foreign country

intolerable (in-TOL-ur-uh-buhl) unbearable

legislature (LEJ-iss-lay-chur) the part of government that is responsible for making and changing laws

massacre (MAS-uh-kur) the violent killing of a large number of people at the same time

militia (muh-LISH-uh) a group of people who are trained to fight but aren't professional soldiers

molasses (muh-LAS-is) a thick, dark, sweet syrup made when sugarcane is processed into sugar

Parliament (PAR-luh-muhnt) the part of the British government that makes laws

rebellion (ri-BEL-yuhn) a struggle against the people in charge of a government

repealed (ri-PEELD) canceled or done away with officially

revenue (REV-uh-noo) the money that a government gets from taxes and other sources

smuggling (SMUHG-uhl-ing) importing goods illegally

treason (TREE-zuhn) the crime of betraying one's own country

wharves (WORVS) long platforms, built along a shore, where boats and ships can load and unload

INDEX

Page numbers in *italics* indicate illustrations.

ABOUT THE AUTHOR

Kevin Cunningham has written more than 40 books on disasters, the history of disease, Native Americans, and other topics. Cunningham lives near Chicago with his wife and their young daughter.